I0412201

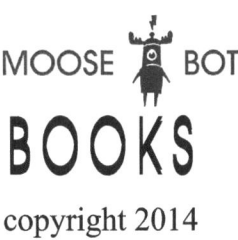

MOOSE BOT

BOOKS

copyright 2014

Dedicated to Ana who taught me
that life in many ways is full of wonder

If I were an octopus

It would be anything but monotonous (mon-ot-on-ous)

Living on the ocean floor

I could roam around and explore!

Having eight arms

Should definitely be one of my charms

Oh yes, super strong arms would be great

Because I could grab up to a hundred times my weight

Plus being a very smart invertebrate (in-vert-e-brate)

I think is also cause to celebrate

And even though I'd be one of about 200,000
(two hundred thousand) eggs that hatch

I'd have suction cups and legs that detach

Of course I could grow them back

Because it's a great defense if under attack

Then with my siphon to swim and ink to spray

I could also change colors and shapes to get away

Both my cousin the squid and I have three hearts

A venomous (ven-om-ous) bite and other similar parts

Some say I have tentacles, like the squid

I don't, but sometimes I wish I did

Not quite three hundred kinds of octopods are known

The smallest, is Wolfi--
                    just half an inch wide when full grown

Then there is the Giant Pacific kind

As much as 150 pounds and 18 feet
from the front to behind

If I were an octopus in the great blue sea

I'd hunt for fish and clams and crabs so tasty to me

With no bones really to speak

My only solid part would be my beak

Allowing me to squeeze into a very tight space

I could bend and twist making a quite silly face

Too bad my life would be so quick

I wouldn't have time to really get sick

Six months to five years at most

I wonder if I could swim the ocean as a ghost?

Probably not, so I guess that's why I will stay

On dry land... at least for today

www.ingramcontent.com/pod-product-compliance
Lightning Source LLC
Chambersburg PA
CBHW060817290526
45792CB00005BB/1699